I0407549

Daily Inspiration: 365 quotes of daily medicine for the mind, body and spirit

Introduction

Every 31st of December, we get truly laser-focused about what the year ahead should look like. We mourn what we didn't achieve in the year that's about to be put to rest, and we step into the mindset of the newness, the possibilities, and the endless plans ahead.

I have come to realize that we cannot relive nor catch what's behind us. However, we can chase the dreams in front of us.

I have also learned that the dreams ahead need not be chased, achieved, or realized through any large miracle. Instead, we just need to believe, have a mindset shift, decide to become a revolutionary change agent, and step out in faith.

Many may find this a challenge—that is ok, too. You see, the reason only a small minority become extraordinary is because of this exact reason; they have been able to make a decision to achieve difference.

This book has come to you from a place of mindset mastery, vision, hope, a decision to shift my own reality, and my refusal to accept that life I was given.

Having grown up in a small rural area of Jamaica—where there wasn't enough to motivate, inspire, or encourage me—I set out to be on a mission of wanting difference, but truly uncertain of what that should look like. Having sold mangoes on the train, having been homeless, and having been sexually assaulted and raped at gunpoint by a total stranger, I decided that I needed to rewrite my story and shape a new narrative for myself—but even moreso for my children and as a result here I am; not just on my own, but with one of my "whys"—my beautiful, talented and resilient daughter Chardonae Elizabeth by my side.

We hope our daily inspirations will help to shape, reshape, and direct your days, and that through these albeit small affirmations your life may become a better version of that which you intend it to be.

If by a stroke of luck you enjoy this book, please don't hesitate to write feedback, share, review, and recommend it.

Lots of love, life, appreciation and abundance.

Ava and Char.

Sending Doves of Gratitude:

I am truly grateful for the life of this warrior of a daughter Chardonae; she has travelled a journey more than her current 18 years in this space. Baby, thanks for weathering the many storms and staying intact as best as you could have. Thanks for the inspiration and courage you have displayed especially in your teenage years. I love you and feel truly blessed to have you as a daughter.

To my son Mikhel Kai—oh baby, you have brought me so much love, laughter, and joy in some of the hardest points in my adult life. I am so much more convinced you were sent as a special blessing out of my storms. Keep that cheeky yet beautiful smile, as it warms my heart each time.

My Cover Designer: Filip Grzincic: your attention to detail in this process was second to none. I appreciate you.

Dario Pirjak: Your guidance and left-brainer mentality are just so important for my growth. Though I don't always agree and occasionally run off with my right-brainer self, I know the true value of having you in my corner.

Jean-Marie Thompson: All I can say is that I know how much you love and pray for me daily, that the love is mutual.

About the Authors

AVA EAGLE BROWN

I am Multi-award winning International Speaker, Author, Life & Business Strategist as well as book coach. I am Dr Ava Eagle Brown I am the author of my memoir The Mango Girl, Bamboo & Fern just name a few of my published books. I have been featured in Financial Times, The Huffington Post and The Voice -UKs Leading Black Newspaper, just to name a few of the press that has sought to have words from this great country girl turned corporate queen. I have managed to use my mindset to PURPOSEWALK from incest, rape, failed marriages and being homeless to a household name globally. My journey has taken on over 4 continents , during which time I have spoken to audiences of over 10000 and shared stage share with some of the best speakers in the industry such as Dr. Eric Thomas, Lisa Nichols, Nick Vujicic, Andy Harrington, Paul O'Mahony, Darren Winters, Mac Attram, Reena Marla, PaulPreston, Joesph McClendon 3rd and Hollywood and Broadway , Dream Girls star Sheryl Lee Ralph. Out of my journey, I have inspired, ignited, motivated, and transformed many especially women to take action, to stand tall and walk into their grace with pride, ease and self-worth. Over the past 18 months, I have helped over 28 individuals rewrite their stories, some of these authors of having gone on to being featured in media globally and have started their journey of transforming others. Why not catch me on my Podcast" The Purposewalk Podcast", where I interview thought leaders walking in their purpose. Subscribe at www.avaeaglebrown.com

I operate on an ethos of transformation through mindset mastery. I seek to empower others to understand that the word IMPOSSIBLE means I"M POSSIBLE - thus helping them claim the lives they were meant to live, a life of abundance, joy, peace and success. The love, desire, and passion I have to see others come out of the RUT and claim their best self, which stands at the CORE of my WHY. My style of being truly transparent, authentic, enthusiastic and welcoming are all part of my success. I believe in NO FLUFF- I have often times been referred to the UK's answer to Lisa Nichols Oprah Winfrey-two women I admire immensely so an honour. I am a book coach the author of the following books: The Mango Girl, Bamboo & Fern, The Journey To Purpose, The Musings & Thoughts of Ava Brown and 30 Steps to a More Fulfilled Life. More can be found at:www.avaeaglebrown.com, Facebook: Dr Ava Eagle Brown, Twitter @avabrown24

CHARDONAE ELIZABETH STEPHENSON (CHAR)

Chardonae was born in Jamaica and migrated to the UK at the tender age of 3 years old. She has studied has always loved music and plays the keyboard, saxophone, drums and guitar. Her love for music has seen her taken up music production at a very popular university in London.Beleive it or not, this is her third time being published, her other works can be found in Young writers of London. Watch out for her music in a few years to come.

I will use my mind to imagine, my heart to believe, and all my might to achieve the success I desire and deserve!

Today I have a strong and positive mental attitude that will attract wonders and miracles into my life!

The struggle that I am overcoming **today is the price I am willing to pay** for my success **tomorrow!**

I know that falling down is not failure because I will always get up. This is an essential part of my success, so I welcome my falls.

I will not surrender the right to define my own life. I choose my own positive actions, which will define my life so that my footsteps are ordered by my maker.

Pressure either bursts pipes or makes diamonds. I am a diamond! I refuse to let pressure break me; instead, it will help me make something priceless.

Today I will plant good seeds **in the good ground so I will reap a good harvest. If I plant good seeds** I will reap my harvest!

I understand that barriers, hurdles, and stumbling blocks may be in my path, so I will be prepared to go around, over, under or through them if necessary!

I will not judge myself based on my past failures. Instead, I will press forward toward the high mark of my purpose. Therein lies my future, my peace, my grace, and my success!

I know that after the storm comes, the rainbow and the sunshine follow. Therefore, I know that after tribulations, tests and trials come peace, happiness, success, joy and blessings!

I will not allow myself to be substandard, nor will I accept substandard results.

To hell with the conditions! I will make opportunities happen **regardless of my circumstances because I am in control of my path and mindset!**

I am a star and I will always shine—even in the life's darkest moments.

My destiny is shaped in the moments where belief and emotion connect!

I never lose. I simply learn what isn't working, and then take the next best course of action. It's not over until I win!

"I am possible"
because
I believe in me!

I remember God bringing me out before, so I do not doubt that he's doing it again now!

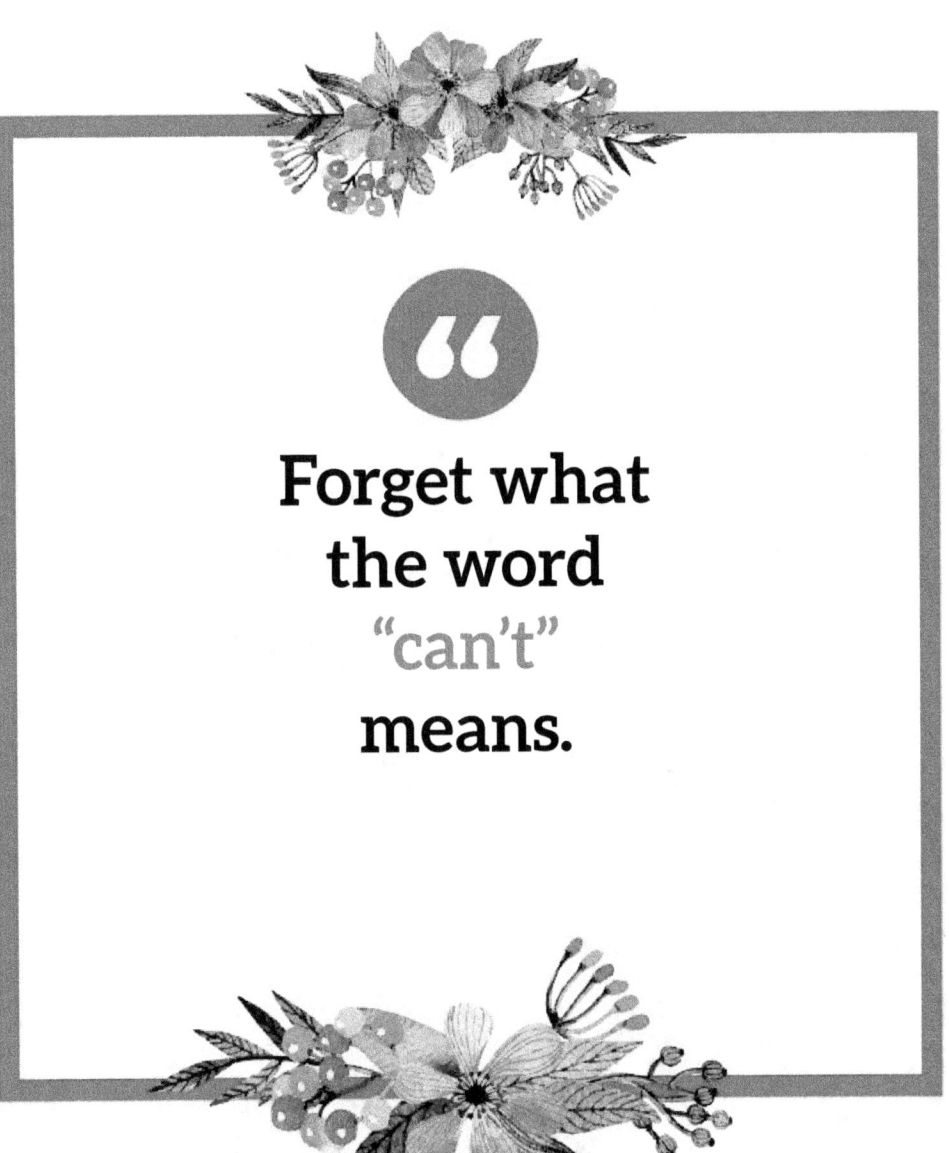

" "

Forget what
the word
"can't"
means.

Every step on the stairway to success is worth it! So, today, I will take triple steps.

I will succeed because I have a will to succeed — and because you haters think I won't.

It's not my first time out of my comfort zone and it won't be my last.

There is a symbiotic relationship between choices and results.

I have learned to see and feel the sun shining, even on a cloudy day.

When I feel like quitting, I remember why I started and that I'll reach my destination if I just keep on moving.

The most inspirational feeling will be achieving my ultimate potential, thus accomplishing my goals.

I will be quick to observe what is not working in my life and begin doing more things that are working by finding new ideas and constantly improving myself.

Every day I wake up **and am given the chance to open my eyes. I will use this day to get closer to** accomplishing my life's purpose.

I am the person I proposed and desired to be!

If I stumble or fall, I will quickly recover and regain my composure, determine my next course of action, and start implementation. My fall cannot and will not hold me back.

I will appreciate what I have learned from past mistakes, but will not overly dwell on what I did wrong.

Since we regret the shots and chances we don't take, I will take the shots and opportunities that support my mission, my purpose, and my assignment!

L.I.F.E. Stands for
Live It Fully Every Day.
So, do just that!

I take ownership and responsibility for the greater "me"—that which I am becoming!

I will give unto others out of the goodness of all that I am, and it will give me all of my goodness in return!

I know that change is constant, so I will be flexible in bending—but I will never break. I will accept the things I cannot change, courageously change what I can, and mold them towards my goals and the betterment of my person.

Tidal waves began as small ripples in the water. At times I may be a ripple, but I will also be a powerful tidal wave of greatness and success.

I am powerful
enough to
my destiny.

I will not hold the greatness that exists inside of me hostage! I will not play small to allow anyone to feel big today! There is enough bigs for us all.

Fear is "false evidence appearing real." I have power, so there's no need for fear!

I am blessed because I have learned to be content regardless of my current state.

I gain and use good knowledge and wisdom every day.

I bring love, light, goodness, peace, and joy everywhere I go, and I use those attributes to affect others in a positively powerful way!

No negative energy
will affect me today.

I control and dictate my own healthy, positive, and creative environment.

I am enthusiastic about my living and about my future!

I know what my future holds for me and it is good!

I see my purpose manifesting daily, and manifesting even more powerfully than I imagined.

I know where I have come from. I'm grateful for where I'm at, and I see where I am going. I owe all of this to my Father who strengthens me and increases me daily.

I am the change that I desire to see in my environment and the world around me.

I know that I am great because I am His greatest creation!

I am a blessing to others!
I increase greatness in
others! I influence people
to be greater and go
further in life.

I move like energy; full of awakening and purpose!

I know that not only does God love me, he likes me! Because I do things to please him!

Every day, I kill and destroy the negative parts of myself so that the positive **parts of me** can live strong and free!

I am long suffering in my persistence of my pursuit of my greatness and goals!

I am not competing with anyone. I am working to be better today than the person I was yesterday!

I will not worry about repaying evil with evil. Instead, I will overcome it with good, positively-charged energy and action!

I look at my vision board and see the pictures turning into reality!

I do not and will not worry about anything! I observe, orient, decide, act and push through until my goals are achieved! Persist until success happens.

My true value and worth are not measured by my bank account, but by the value I pour into others and the value I bring to the world. It is the worth of my relational account that holds my true value!

I am not and will not be obsessed with money, but I will have it abundantly.

I will work hard— but I will work twice as smart as I work hard.

I forgive and release those that trespass against me, so that others may forgive me for any pain I may have caused them. I also forgive myself for any decisions that I may have made that I don't feel good about. In this way, I am not bound by any emotional or spiritual bondage or baggage.

I will lift up those that I can, as the Father lifts me up.

I am dedicated to being a positive moving force, as I move positively and progressively forward every day.

Liars are cowards looking to avoid the natural outcome of things through deception. Only the honest are brave enough to accept the consequences. I am brave and I am honest in all that I do.

I do not mind being uncomfortable, but I do mind being unsuccessful. I will practice succeeding in all the assignments that support my mission and my purpose.

I will continuously be bold in my endeavors! Boldness gets recognized. Timidity causes hesitation. I will not waste time or become timid! I am pressing boldly onward to the victory and success that God has set for me and that I desire!

I will not run away in fear from the possibility of failure. I will act wisely and boldly, knowing that success is on the other side of risk!

If things get tough, I get tougher. I will take a moment, **observe, orient, act, and push through!**

"

I will not allow myself to live or feel oppressed. I have a free perspective. Therefore, I have a spirit of freedom and liberty—where the spirit of the Lord is, there is liberty.

Hard tasks have become easy because I aim to do the impossible!

My performance in the uncomfortable zone is critical!

I separate myself from the masses and blaze my own trail! Leaders separate, while followers assimilate.

I know and understand that every tomorrow I am blessed with is a new day filled with new ideas, new opportunities, and new beginnings. I will seize all that I can!

I know that all things are working together for my good, because I love God and I am walking in his called purpose for my life.

Being in itself is reason enough to prosper.
All intentions should aspire to the condition of solace.

The strength of will **alone can prevail.**

Active self-knowledge is the worthiest goal.

Conquering your fears is the path to true self-worth.

As long as the course is freely held, it cannot fail to reward.

Nothing can have greater value that an honest pursuit.

When compelled, every single eventuality will be mastered.

In accepting life's challenges, readiness is all.

Nothing can deter from the ultimate purpose.

To strive to cleanse the inviolate unconquerable soul.

Whatever is accomplished shall be what is intended.

Nothing will dissuade from a righteous objective.

Rational positivism
is the most
sanguine approach.

Great expectations **yield even** greater outcomes.

Achieving success is relatively neutral.

When the attempt is all, the result shall be all.

Every experience
can yield an answer
to another.

The uncluttered mind is primed for success.

Only a pure soul can yield a tranquil mind.

I will not get angry when I fail or fall down. But I most certainly will refuse to stay down. I will always get up, and I will always rise up!

Remember, liars are cowards looking to avoid the natural outcome of things through deception—only the honest are brave enough to accept the consequences.

What is the point of living a comfortable life? The harder the challenges you overcome, the stronger you become.

Live every day to make sure you do something **by the end of it to get yourself a satisfying sleep.**

Awakening

The idea of these inspirations is to offer you daily empowering words, phrases or even sentences that will inspire, motivate, encourage, strengthen, energise, influence, ignite activate and create lasting change in all areas of life throughout the year -hence we have 365 daily quotes. Through the repetition of affirmations positive mental images are created in the conscious and subconscious mind, which in turn- affect behaviour, actions, decisions, feelings and a lot more. Daily quotes we hope, will make help you find it permissible to become more intentional, add clarity and intently direct your mind, body and soul towards a purpose-driven day, week, month and eventually year. No matter at what stage you are at in life, you can use affirmations to ignite and direct the changes you want, are entitled to and need in your life. Being happy and at peace are parts of your God-given birthright.

There is no formula for success. Each and every one of us have that one opportunity to make it into the stratosphere. Make it count.

We can't eliminate evil from this planet. All we can do is fight the good fight. Without evil there is no good.

It's never too late
to pursue what you
always wanted to.

Yes, hard work is a desirable trait—but smart work will fetch you the same results for the least amount of work possible.

Don't fear death. Many of the world's defining moments came under circumstances where lesser men would have scuttled to save their hinds.

Never run away from failure. If you fall, get back up and dust yourself off. Then, grab the bull by the horns and wrestle him down.

When life gets tougher and things aren't working as easily as they used to, just think you're in a video game—you probably just levelled up.

DAY 107

Living like a beggar is appreciated who wanders independently, rather than an emperor tied to a seat oppressed by others.

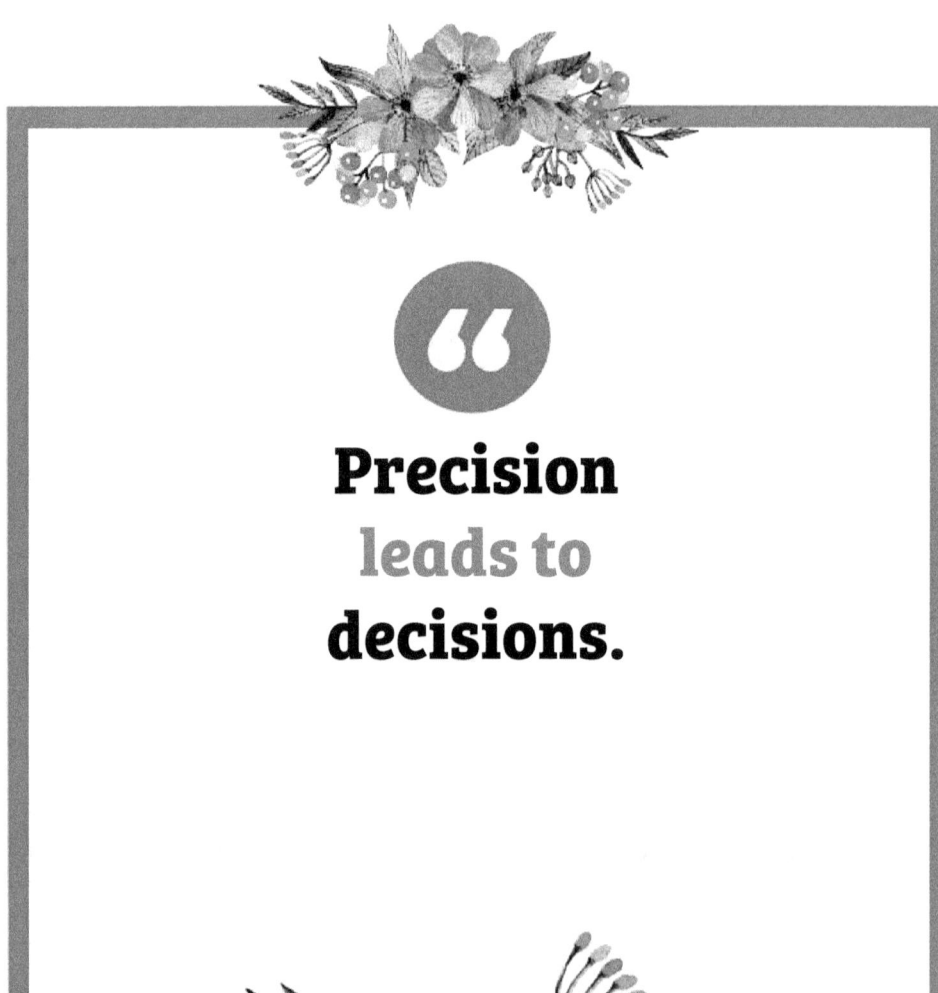

Precision
leads to
decisions.

Some prove their worth
by keeping busy.
Others just make it
purposeful.

Life is about making
an impression,
not depression.

You are just missing the shots you are not taking.

Life isn't about conceiving and receiving, it's give and take.

We are what
we feel
intrinsically.

Every trigger I pull is taking me closer to my aim.

The real thing is acting upon your decisions; the rest is just determination.

The wind in my opposite direction gives me the true picture to build my future.

I welcome challenges because they make me stronger.

I read my competitors so as not to repeat their mistakes and to learn from their successes.

I am glad that later I realized my
strength is me.

My dog taught me to be loyal to my master.

To be on a learning curve is the key to an unbeatable competitive advantage.

If you do not have something to achieve when you get up, go to back to sleep.

We become what we
want to become.

Success is how fast you get up every time you fall.

You will not regret the things you did that went wrong, **but you will** regret the things you did not try.

Today is your treasure, so live it fully.

You only fail if you give up, so never give up.

Only you are responsible for what you become.

If you want to get something, start giving it from today.

The only thing that lives forever is change, so learn to embrace change.

Every great thing started small, so do not worry and take a start.

You have tremendous potential to learn, fight, and shine. Believe in yourself.

I am living against all the odds; I will continue to do so.

You cannot live to the fullest unless something is killing you inside.

I am blessed that all my body parts are without any disabilities, for which I am thankful.

Fear vanishes **if you choose to face it.**

The more you give, the more you get.
Try it.

Everyone is blessed
differently—so am I,
and so you are.

The world needs kindness.
Be Kind.

To love is to give.

If you want to see a change in the world, change yourself.

Change comes
from the inside out.

Be your own best friend. Listen to what your best friend says.

If you want to be lucky,
work hard.

Yesterday is not ours to recover, but tomorrow is ours to win or lose.

Always keep your eyes and your ears open— there is so much to come.

If you want something bad enough, the world comes to your side.

Appreciate the person you see in the mirror every day.

Be thankful for every
new sun you see.

No one can beat you if you are persistent.

We concentrate more on the things which are not than the things which are.

Love yourself.
Respect yourself.
And be your own hero.

The more you fail, the more you develop.

Everyone has their own blessings, their own doubts, their own fears, **and their own failures—do not compare yourself to anyone.**

You are unique and exclusive; you are the only version of your kind.

You must know exactly what you want to get exactly what you deserve.

Good luck **comes only if you** overcome bad luck. **Stay steadfast and resolute.**

Stop wishing for the good things. Instead, take action and the good things will find their way to you.

People will treat you the way you treat yourself.

People know you through you.

Live as much as you can; there is no limit.

Do not waste your days worrying. Make the most happiness out of every day.

The **greatest skill** a man can learn is how to tackle different situations without losing himself.

A minute of negativity takes weeks to cure. Think positively.

Forgive others
as you
forgive yourself.

You are the best thing
that ever happened to
you.

Failure is a milestone of success.

You are much more than your shortcomings.

Lift others if you want to lift yourself.

Dream, resolve and stick to it.

Keep moving—
for it is the only
way to survive.

Be your own team.

Life isn't always about winning—it's more about living.

Escape into your own soul and explore who you are more often.

Purpose Walking

At times when life feels tough, misfortune visits, your luck runs out or your esteem has been battered, inspirations of daily quotes can be used to banish depression, revitalise your soul, redirect your energies and accomplish your, dreams, desires wants and needs. From seemingly trivial matters to heart-wrenching traumas daily quotes and affirmations are the silent companions that rebuild your fortitude and lead you towards a life enriched with joy, success, happiness and all that you desire. This book of quotes can help you cross the tracks that made you feel like you would S.I.N.K and instead help you S.O.A.R.

Embrace all your experiences. They were necessary.

Refuse to believe others' opinions of who you are. It's your opinion that counts.

Your smile can be the cure to someone's day, so start smiling every day.

Learn to walk **when something—anything— doesn't feel good in your gut.**

Don't compromise to be recognized regardless of what the prize is.

Stop measuring your life based on your path.

Your humble beginnings can be a great platform for your greatness.

Upgrade your thoughts to upgrade your life.

Free yourself from your own self critic.

Today be the gift you
want someone to offer
you; be your own rescue.

Inhale the weariful air and that is all you embody.

Learn to accept that your experiences were all necessary; they are your teacher.

Knowing your worth helps you realize how special you are.

Today, replace the past with new possibilities.

Create new experiences starting today with your thoughts—be open to new creation.

Learn to sit in your power by resting in your awareness.

Release the past and move into your abundant future.

I am prepared for this moment.

I am totally enough; I won't need anything outside of me to make me whole.

Quote yourself thinking - what would it be in writing? Make sure your thoughts are ones you are happy to write down.

There are many victories in every try.

Today's skies may be grey, but focus on the forecast.

Live your story today; read it tomorrow.

Freedom comes from

success and failure.

There are many hands you can be dealt; strategy is key.

Aim to be remembered like great myths echoed from lips.

Respect the training and one day become the trainer.

Challenges breed successful people.

This time is not different.

But you are!

You will become thankful for the trial that made you new, and for the lessons that were learned when you were forced to see them through.

Be you, bravely.

Your integrity to your goals in planted in nurtured soil, growing beyond your fields.

In facing challenges, you learn new things **about you and life.**

Many are looking for signs; others are creating them.

You are your words, and your words are your strength.

You are your empire; keep building you.

Inspiration:
found everywhere.

Do something great today that justifies yesterday and promises a better tomorrow

Tomorrow's success relies on today's hustle.

Invest in the quality of transparency—you may not see it now, but it will pay off later.

Sometimes you have to lose to win.

Find your own measurements; there is no balance in the scales of success and failure.

Picture the future. **If you are not smiling in the future, then your perspective is out of focus.**

I respect those who are passionate— sometimes, passion is all it takes.

When you make a ground investment, you will never worry about your foundation.

Never fear to create and recreate every day.

See the positivity in both the rise and the fall.

Every sacrifice you make now will be worth it later.

At some point, you will only be a step away from making your dreams your reality.

Stability is feeling like you are soaring through clouds despite having your feet on the ground.

Build today, enjoy tomorrow.

See the individual pixels,
but never lose sight of
the big picture.

They say to aim for the moon and fall short among the stars. But I was not made to miss.

No matter the case, you owe it to yourself to try one more time.

The objective of every day should be to adapt.

Allow absolutely nothing to separate you from the reality of success.

You create your future. Wake up and make those better choices today.

Celebrate
your beginning,
your middle,
and your end.

You are all the inspiration you will ever need.

With unique DNA in your veins, you can never lack authenticity.

Every answer we search for is hidden behind the right question.

Enjoy the journey.

Never forget to water your creativity.

Whether you stand or fall is a choice only you have the right to make.

If you want to make the change, then you need to make the change.

Be better today and greater tomorrow.

Effort and energy are the currency you use for hard work to pay off.

DAY 242

You can hear success if you block your ears and listen to your heart.

Every victory is
worth the fight.

Let your
confidence shine.

Each time you see the sunset, count your victories.

Hold firm to success; it is found within.

Stop counting the number of times you've fall down, and instead count the number of times you've gotten back up.

Be courageous.
Be Brave and Be Bold.

Your story only has one writer.

Leave behind the worthless, and attain something priceless.

Become the
difference.

I've watched a lot of ordinary people become successful; the real magic happened when I stopped watching and became.

Success is like a little fire constantly burning within, waiting to become a blaze.

If I told you effort is the secret ingredient, would you be brave enough to write your own recipe for a happy soul?

Tomorrow is an
empty canvas.

The success of your work relies on your attitude towards it.

You will like what you do when your head is in it, but love what you do when your heart is in it.

Sometimes you have to go the distance to make the difference.

Think of yourself as not just a wonderful creation, but also as a creator.

Purpose makes it possible.

Whenever life questions you, be ready to answer.

The first step to finishing is starting.

The success of failure: continue with a smile.

Silence the doubts.

Exist in the now and live in the now.

Find tomorrow and
bury yesterday.

Each day comes with its own triumphs.

Passion is displayed on the outside but begins within.

The more responsibility you have, the more trust others have put in you.

Hoping will help you take first steps, but believing will make you fly.

You can if you have the will to do it. So just decide and execute.

The true definition of work: An activity involving mental or physical effort done in order to achieve a result.

Questions
increase
knowledge.

Find the reason, **and then make it make you succeed!**

Igniting

I have used daily affirmations throughout my adult years to help me grow even when all I was doing was just repeating them. Overtime they became words I started believing an ultimately lived by. Affirmations and daily quotes have become a huge part of my daily routine and are embedded in who I am. Best of all, affirmation can be used at anytime and anywhere. Whether silently spoken whilst you're cooking, ironing, these days even when I step on stage or meet with someone influential, I use them silently to keep me calm. They can be repeated in your mind as you work or shouted at the top of your lungs they are always effective, comforting, encouraging and empowering. Try using some when you are at that stressful job you hate, or in a quarrel–instead of blowing your top affirm silently. Chardonae and I hope that this book will allow you to truly understand and experience the profound impact that affirmations have in every area of life despite your current circumstance or unfortunate situation. Do enjoy and share you feedback with us. Remember: Life is not always easy and it's not always fair but through affirmations, you can reset and rejuvenate your life in your favour and achieve everything you've ever dreamed of and more.

The greatest teacher is our trials.

Every path leads to a destination—walk yours with pride.

Here is your moment to close your eyes, dig deep, and truly give it your all.

Your integrity to your goals is planted in nurtured soil, growing beyond your fields.

Grow, slay, and pray.

Stand in the mirror and confidently repeat: "The power in me is stronger than what mere eyes can see."

Your words assume people are listening, but your actions are all they hear.

Capture and share beautiful moments.

Be a living Polaroid.

Never fear to create and
recreate every day.

You can hear success is something enjoyed, felt within.

No battle is too big to be won.

There is always a
reason to smile.

You are a wordsmith by nature.

Enjoy the beautiful.

Your focus today will render tomorrow's reward.

Your questions will breed your wisdom.

Every "thank you," "well done," and "I am sorry" affects the heart.

Become that which you were meant to be.

Identify what drives you, then no longer fight its control.

I am my own rescue and will dictate my path today.

Every day is a gift to me, and I won't waste anymore of this gift.

Grace, favor, and success comes to me naturally.

I deserve the best of today; it's a day laced with endless possibilities.

Forgiveness is the open door I will walk through from this day onwards.

Relationships are built on trust. Once that is broken, it's difficult to mend.

Stop, smell the fresh air, and expand your lungs.

We all have a choice every day—so choose wisely.

The less you stress, the better you feel—you can't choose the day of the week, but you can choose not to be stressed.

You can't choose how you were born. However, the way you die can be a choice you make starting today.

Declutter your space and declutter your life—your environment affects your emotional state.

Challenges are platforms for growth and greatness.

The mind is the most powerful, yet fragile, weapon you possess.

Each moment is priceless. **There is no replay button on life, so take each breath carefully.**

Fear is the universe telling us there is success behind its tail.

There are no coincidences in life; every action has a purpose—you just need to look hard enough.

Insanity is in all of us. However, sanity also exists in all of us. Daily, it's a choice we all have to make to be sane or insane.

Don't get frustrated when things go wrong—pause, and think.

Relationships are bank accounts, so try to deposit rather than just withdraw.

Choose **happiness, joy, and peace today.**

Affirm with me: "I am enough; I am enough."

Taste what you say today, and if the flavor isn't pleasant than take a note to think before you speak.

Crying can release pain and help you see clearly, so don't be afraid to cry.

Meandering roads can have smooth endings, but you have to stay on the path to discover the end.

Release all the past and
inhale your breathtaking
possibilities.

All wounds are healed with time, love, and tenderness. Be tender to yourself; don't wait for someone to be tender to you.

The body, mind, and spirt are all connected. You can't look after one and not the other; it's a holistic approach.

Healing starts with you--don't wait for the other person.

Sometimes, we have to be tossed and turned to be laced into our **greatness**—enjoy being tossed and turned.

When in the midst of a challenge, focus on the lessons to be learned.

Being authentic is your greatest perfume; wear it daily.

Don't hide **behind what makes you comfortable.**

You can directly measure life by the will to endure, persevere, and survive.

Sometimes, your life has to be turned upside down and rebuilt in an effort to find your God-given place.

Sometimes we go through life feeling broken—then one simple, magical thing can happen to change that course, Hold on for your magical moment.

True identity is hard for some of us, and leads us to question our identity—however, true identity is knowing who you are for yourself.

Shifting

I have used daily affirmations throughout my adult years to help me grow even when all I was doing was just repeating them. Overtime they became words I started believing and ultimately lived by. Affirmations and daily quotes have become a part huge of my daily routine and are embedded in who I am.

Best of all, affirmation can be used at anytime and anywhere. Whether silently spoken whilst you're cooking, ironing, these days even when I step on stage or meet with someone influential , I use them silently to keep me calm . They can be repeated in your mind as you work or shouted at the top of your lungs, they are always effective, comforting, encouraging and empowering. Try using some when you are at that stressful job you hate, or in a quarrel –instead of blowing your top affirm silently.

Chardonae and I hope that this book will allow you to truly understand and experience the profound impact that affirmations have on every area of life despite your current circumstance or unfortunate situation. Do enjoy and share you feedback with us.

Remember : Life is not always easy and it's not always fair but through affirmations you can reset and rejuvenate your life in your favor and achieve everything you've ever dreamed of and more.

Love, Ava & Char

Most of us are not afraid of the dark—we are afraid of the truth that lies within it.

Even without recognition, in the coldest parts of us fear burns from conception until we decide to stare it in the face.

Disappointments are appointments set by God.

Stop running from that which you fear. **Stand**, and see where you end up.

Don't run from the waves
—ride the tides.

Become a hunter.
That way, you will avoid being hunted.

A broken heart is the start of loving like you have never been hurt.

Your weaknesses
are hidden strengths.

The ability to get up one last time makes you the champion of your own destiny.

Our greatest fear is that
we can move mountains
with our minds if we dare
ourselves to try.

Take time out for you today—**shut down and disappear from the chaos.**

There is never a bad decision; there is always a new lesson learned.

All your experiences have been valuable.

The sadness you feel today will eventually be erased with hope, joy, and peace—you just have to give yourself time.

Every person on your journey is relevant.

Cultivate a spirt of
allowing.

Don't stand in your own way.

Stop explaining yourself to everyone. Get up, bounce, and slay.

Today, affirm that you are unapologetically awesome.

Be your biggest cheerleader and everyone else will have to follow.

Do not be afraid to drop the homies in order to grow.

Forgiveness doesn't let the perpetrator off the hook; it frees you and imprisons them.

Arise and become the awesomeness that you were born to be—take your power back.

Don't run after things that are leaping away from you. There is a reason for all occurrences.

Someone else's opinion of you doesn't have to define you. The only person's opinion of you that matters is you

Life is short, so live every day like it's golden.

Smile—it's such wonderful therapy.

Seekers reap. Become a seeker and reap your rewards.

At the end of pain, there is a heap of success.

You have to stop letting yourself down. Instead, start executing and give it everything you have.

Look yourself in the mirror and be happy with who you see.

Don't make a permanent decision **based on a** temporary feeling.

Embrace all that life throws at you. Every experience in life—the good, the bad, and the ugly—shapes us into the best versions of ourselves.

Stay focused on your goals. Life has a funny way of throwing you off track, but you may find the essentials on the dirt road instead of on one someone has already paved.

Ignore the smoke and focus on outing the fire; **life has minor challenges that are made from a deeper source**

Appreciation will aid in your elevation: value and earn to manipulate what you already have so you can obtain your desires.

> "Feeling small and being
> small is all
> a matter of attitude.
> You are exactly who
> you think you are;
> good or bad.
> Think more of yourself.
> **THINK BIGGER!**"

AVA *Eagle* BROWN